A CAMBRIDGE TOPIC BOOK

The Parthenon

Susan Woodford

Published in cooperation with Cambridge University Press
Lerner Publications Company, Minneapolis

LIBRARY OF CONGRESS CATALOGING IN PUBLICATION DATA

Woodford, Susan.
The Parthenon.

(A Cambridge topic book)
"Published in cooperation with Cambridge University
Press."
Includes index.
Summary: An account of the design, building, decora-
tion, and eventual destruction of the temple dedicated
to Athena, and aspects of Greek life and worship.
1. Parthenon (Athens, Greece)—Juvenile literature.
[1. Parthenon (Athens, Greece)] I. Title.
NA281.W64 1983   726'.1208'09385   82-25878
ISBN 0-8225-1128-9 (lib. bdg.)

This edition first published 1983 by Lerner Publications Company
by permission of Cambridge University Press.

Original edition copyright © 1981 by Cambridge University Press
as part of *The Cambridge Introduction to the History of Mankind: Topic Book.*

International Standard Book Number: 0-8225-1228-9
Library of Congress Catalog Card Number: 82-25878

Manufactured in the United States of America

This edition is available exclusively from:
Lerner Publications Company, 241 First Avenue North, Minneapolis, Minnesota 55401

1 2 3 4 5 6 7 8 9 10 92 91 90 89 88 87 86 85 84 83

Contents

Three gods carved in low relief, from the east frieze of the Parthenon.

1 How the Parthenon came to be built

The Persian wars

Late in the summer of 490 BC the Persian fleet sailed along the Athenian coast and landed an army on the plain of Marathon.

The Athenians had been expecting it. Nine years earlier the Greek city-states in Asia Minor had rebelled against the rule of the Persian king and had begged for help from their brothers in mainland Greece. Athens and nearby Eretria had sent aid. Within five years the Persians crushed the revolt; then they turned their attention to punishing the Greek cities that had supported the rebels. Now Eretria had fallen and it looked as though Athens would be next.

The Persian forces vastly outnumbered the small Athenian army that marched out, accompanied by 1000 men from the allied city of Plataea, to face them.

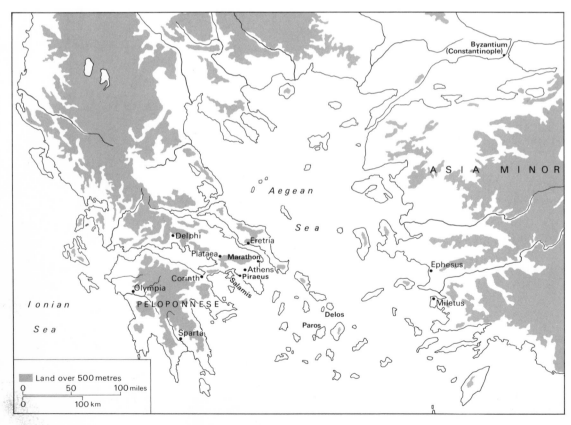

1.1 Greek city-states, sanctuaries, and battle sites mentioned in this book are indicated on the map. The ancient Greeks lived not only on mainland Greece (left) and the islands of the Aegean (centre), but also along the coast of Asia Minor (right) and in Sicily and South Italy (not shown). During the sixth century BC those living to the east had been absorbed into the empire of the Persians.

The Athenians had only two things in their favour: a well-trained body of heavily armed foot soldiers (1.2) and a passionate love for freedom. When the battle was joined, the Persians broke through the Athenian centre, but the wings held firm and finally closed in on the more lightly armed Persians in a pincer movement. At the end of the day 192 Athenians had fallen, but 6400 Persians lay dead on the field.

The Athenian victory seemed the more glorious for having been so unexpected. The Athenians were immensely proud; the Persians were immensely angry. They swore they would avenge the humiliation that they had suffered, but it was ten years before the Persians launched another attack.

In the moment of their triumph the Athenians decided to build a splendid new temple on the south side of their acropolis. *Acropolis* means 'high city'. The acropolis at Athens was a large flat-topped rock that was accessible only from the west, as you can see at the bottom left of the aerial view on page 1. It had originally been the citadel – a fortress – but had eventually come to be reserved as a sanctuary for the worship of the gods. The new temple was probably intended not only as a thank-offering to the goddess Athena, who the

1.2 The disciplined ranks of foot soldiers who won the battle of Marathon fought in formations much like the ones painted on a vase 150 years earlier.

Athenians believed had helped them to gain their victory, but also as a memorial to the men who had fought and died to win it. The building project was still in its early stages when the Persians returned in full force in 480 BC. This time they succeeded in invading Athens, sacking the city, and burning all the buildings on the acropolis, including the beginnings of the new temple.

The conquest of Athens was part of a massive invasion of Greece by land and sea. The Greeks lived in independent city-states and were usually busy squabbling among themselves. Now most of them united to face the Persian menace. But the Persians swept all before them. When it became clear that Athens could not be defended, the Athenians, after evacuating all those unable to fight, left everything – homes and temples, fields and orchards – to climb aboard their ships and carry on the war at sea.

Their courage was rewarded, for through skill and daring they enabled the Greeks to smash the Persian fleet in the bay of Salamis. The next year, under the leadership of Sparta, the city with the finest army, the united Greeks defeated the Persians on land near Plataea. On the battlefield of Plataea the Greeks took an oath not to rebuild the temples that the Persians had destroyed, but to leave them in ruins, eternal testimony to the Persians' impiety.

Athens had been destroyed, but not the Athenians. Once again the people had triumphed, though at a terrible cost. When the Athenians returned to their devastated country, they set the damaged remains of the columns of the partly built temple into the walls of the acropolis (1.3) as a sort of war

memorial. They placed them so that they could be seen from the *agora*, the civic and commercial centre of the city. There they have remained to this day.

The Delian League becomes an Athenian empire

The victories in 480 and 479 BC were followed up on land and sea, and the Greek cities on the coast of Asia Minor were liberated from Persia. Nevertheless the people living in coastal and island cities were afraid of the Persians, who were still very powerful. They therefore bound themselves together in a league, with each city agreeing to help to maintain a navy strong enough to keep the Persians in check. The Athenians, who had the largest fleet, were asked to act as leaders. The other city-states, who were all independent, contributed ships or money according to what they could afford as assessed by Aristeides, an Athenian celebrated for his fairness. Meetings were held on Delos. The sanctuary of the god Apollo on this mid-Aegean island was a religious centre particularly sacred to the Ionians, a branch of the Greek people to which most of the allied cities belonged. The league treasury was placed under the protection of Apollo and the league came to be called the Delian League. Eventually most cities chose to provide money instead of ships, on the understanding that Athens would use the money to equip a navy strong enough to discourage the Persians from making any attack. The Athenians gladly agreed to this.

Time passed.

After a while some of the members of the Delian League tried to behave independently; they soon discovered that they could no longer do so. Athens, grown vastly in strength, forced them back into the alliance. Little by little it became clear that the Delian League was turning into an Athenian empire. In 454 BC the Athenians had the League treasury transferred from Delos to Athens, where it came under the protection of the goddess Athena and where it remained as long as the empire lasted.

In the meantime, the Athenians rebuilt their city and erected long walls to connect it with the port at Piraeus a little over 6 kilometres (about 4 miles) away. After the Persian sack, Piraeus was reconstructed according to a simple geometrical layout, with straight streets crossing at right angles and special areas reserved for housing, trade and religion. Any attempt to impose such a rational plan on the city of Athens itself failed. People were happy to return to their homes after the war and longed to recreate the city as it had been. They rebuilt their houses along the same narrow, winding lanes that had been used before. The houses themselves were modest affairs, sturdily though irregularly built out of sun-dried mud-brick. There was nothing very grand about them. In fact there was very little in the way of grand architecture.

Much of the public life of the Athenians consisted of large outdoor gatherings of people. Citizens congregated to attend the Assembly (the ruling body in the Athenian democracy) or to participate in religious festivals (which often included athletic events or dramatic performances). An open space with a platform for the speakers was all that was needed for the Assembly, and hillsides were used as natural grandstands for watching athletic contests or plays. Hardly any striking buildings would have caught the eye of a visitor to the busy and thriving city.

Temples to Greek gods were often built on a monumental scale out of expensive and durable materials like marble. Temples in most Greek cities contrasted with the humble dwellings of the people in much the same way that medieval cathedrals contrasted with the little houses that were clustered around them. But in Athens the temples had not been rebuilt after the Persian destruction. There was no really beautiful and impressive building to demonstrate the importance of the city.

1.4 Portrait of Pericles. The Greek sculptor Kresilas made a full-length statue of Pericles in the fifth century BC. This has not survived, but we can get some idea of what the great statesman looked like from copies that Roman sculptors made of the head alone.

Pericles, the leader of the democracy, must have felt that the glamour of empire was greatly diminished if there was no visible evidence of power and distinction. Around 449 BC Athens had made peace with Persia, and with the war at an end, the oath of Plataea no longer seemed so binding. The time had come, he believed, to rebuild the temples destroyed by the Persians. Pericles therefore persuaded the Athenians to send out heralds with invitations to *all* the Greek city-states – mainland as well as island – that had fought the Persians, to come to a conference at Athens. They were to discuss the rebuilding of the temples and the policing of the seas. This was an important issue for the members of the Delian League, who must have been wondering whether, once peace had been made, they ought to go on making their contributions to the Athenians.

None of the states invited sent delegates. People in other cities had come to resent the growing power of Athens and were afraid that by attending a conference that she had called, they would seem to be giving Athens a position of leadership that not everyone thought she was entitled to. This was particularly true of Sparta and her allies in the Peloponnese, who were not members of the Delian League and who were becoming increasingly jealous of Athens.

Athens, therefore, decided on her own. Not surprisingly the

Athenians concluded that the members of the Delian League should continue to pay tribute-money, if not for defence against Persia, then in order to maintain the freedom of the seas. For one year the money had not been collected; now the collections were resumed.

The decision to build the Parthenon

When it became clear that no conference would be held, Pericles proposed to the Athenian Assembly that a new temple should be built on the site of the one that had been begun after the battle of Marathon. The Assembly, which consisted of all adult male citizens, made all the laws and decisions for the city; it controlled state funds and required those who received them to give a full account of their use. Pericles suggested that the temple should be financed out of state funds which had been increased by a transfer of money from the Delian League. He recommended that the temple should be large enough to contain a statue of Athena of a magnificence never before seen: a gigantic image covered in gold and ivory.

At the same time Pericles proposed that enough money should be set aside to maintain the fleet and add ten new ships every year. He argued that since Athens would provide the navy required by the terms of the Delian League in order to keep control of the sea, she was entitled to use any surplus money as she saw fit. The Assembly voted on the proposals and approved them.

Thus the Athenians decided in 448 BC that the Parthenon should be built. Pericles doubtless intended that its beauty should serve as such stunning testimony to Athens' cultural excellence as to reconcile the world to her increasing power.

Once the Assembly had approved the plan to build the Parthenon, Iktinos and Kallikrates were chosen as architects and the sculptor Phidias, a friend of Pericles, was appointed to make the gold and ivory statue and to be in overall charge of the project. The Assembly, however, maintained its control by appointing a committee of five overseers (*epistatai*) each year while the work was carried on. They kept records of the money voted for the temple and the statue and how it was spent; they were responsible to the Assembly. The Assembly voted the funds at the beginning of each year, and at the end reviewed how they had been spent. After the annual accounts had been approved, they were carved on stone slabs, fragments of which survive to this day. This was the usual procedure when the democratic Assembly of the Athenians undertook a public building project. No changes were made for the erection of the Parthenon.

The Athenian people were pleased with their decision to build the Parthenon. Not only would the temple and its remarkable statue redound to the glory of their city, but the building would also provide employment for many men doing different jobs, paid for out of public funds. Plutarch, in his *Life of Pericles*, vividly describes the veritable army of workers whose skills and labour were required: 'carpenter, modeller, coppersmith, stonemason, dyer, worker in gold and ivory, painter, embroiderer, and engraver, and besides these carriers and suppliers of materials such as merchants, sailors, and pilots for the sea-borne traffic, and waggon-makers, trainers of draught animals, and drivers for everything that came by land. There were also rope-makers, weavers, leatherworkers, road-builders and miners. Each individual craft, like a general with an army under his separate command, had its own corps of unskilled labourers at its disposal, and these worked in a subordinate capacity.'

Before we see how this multitude of workers went about the enormous task of building and decorating the Parthenon, we should pause for a moment to look at how the Greeks worshipped their gods and why they thought a temple should be built at all.

2 How the Greeks worshipped their gods and goddesses

The Greek gods and goddesses

The Greeks believed not in any single, all-powerful god, but in many gods and goddesses who between them controlled the forces of nature and the fate of men.

Zeus was the chief of the gods, the master over thunder and lightning, who gathered the clouds and sent rain. His brother Poseidon was the god of the sea and the lord of earthquakes. Zeus' favourite daughter, Athena, was strong in war and clever in handicrafts. The strange story was told that she had no mother, but sprang fully grown and fully armed from the head of Zeus (2.1). She was the patron goddess of the Athenians.

Athenian legend claimed that Poseidon and Athena had been rivals for the possession of Athens. They had held a contest on the acropolis, the high rock dominating the city (page 1). Poseidon had struck the rock with his trident and caused a salt spring to appear; Athena had plunged her spear into the ground and an olive tree emerged. Olive trees grew particularly well around Athens and played an important part in the economy (2.2). Both the salt spring and the olive tree were considered sacred and, however they may have got there, they were still to be seen on the acropolis in the second century AD.

Greek myths (the stories about gods) were told and retold quite freely. Various traditions arose as different versions of the stories were recounted, and no one version had to be considered better or truer than the others. The myths were not part of a fixed religious system; the Greeks had no holy book like the Bible which is supposed to be the word of God.

According to one tradition the contest between Athena and Poseidon was settled by a vote of the Athenians, while according to another, Zeus was the judge. The two traditions agreed about the outcome: Athena won, and the city consequently took its name from her. The Athenians worshipped her and prayed to her. They felt that her good will had brought

2.1 This painting on a storage jar made in the first half of the fifth century BC shows a tiny Athena, wearing a helmet and carrying a spear, springing from the head of Zeus. Another god, the craftsman Hephaistos, assisted with the birth by splitting Zeus' head with his axe. He is shown here walking off to the left, looking back at his handiwork.

their victories and prosperity and they wished to thank her. They did not neglect the worship of Poseidon or Zeus or any of the other gods – that would have seemed dangerous to them – but they considered Athena their special protector.

The Greeks imagined that their gods and goddesses looked much like human beings and felt and behaved like them as well, though they were thought to be more beautiful and more powerful than men, and free from human ills, such as sickness and death.

Like the Greeks themselves, the gods were supposed to enjoy looking at beautiful things and watching displays of skill. The gods were pleased when statues, representing either the

gods themselves or their worshippers, were dedicated to them or when songs were sung or races run in their honour. Special festivals would be held for them every year, and some were held with unusual splendour every four years.

The most important part of religious worship was the sacrifice of animals accompanied by prayers in honour of the gods. The sacrifices took place at an open-air altar. Altars were essential for worship; nothing else was. Altars existed in sanctuaries long before anything else was built.

All great festivals culminated in the ceremony in which prayers were recited while the fat and bones of the sacrificed animals were burned on the altar as an offering to the gods. The meat was then carefully roasted as a treat for the worshippers (2.3).

The feast shared with the gods was also a very special event for the people, for it was only on rare occasions that the Greeks ate meat. Their usual food consisted of bread, cheese, garlic, onions, beans and olives, with wine for zest and honey for sweetness. Even fish was something of a delicacy (2.4).

The Athenians honoured Athena every year with a festival called the *Panathenaia*. It was celebrated on a summer day that was supposed to be the anniversary of Athena's extra-ordinary birth from her father's head.

Every four years the Panathenaia was celebrated with greater than usual magnificence. There were athletic com-petitions – running, wrestling, boxing, javelin and discus throwing – horse races, ship races, musical competitions and competitions in the recitation of the *Iliad* and the *Odyssey*. At the end of the *Great Panathenaia* (as the quadrennial festival was called) the Athenians also presented their beloved god-dess with a new dress called a *peplos* that had been carefully woven over the last nine months by specially chosen Athenian maidens. The peplos was taken up to the acropolis in a grand procession in which people from all levels of Athenian society participated. The climax of the ceremony was the presentation

left: *2.3 This painting on a bowl used for mixing wine and water made in Athens in the later fifth century BC shows the aftermath of a sacrifice. Meat from the sacrificed animals is being roasted over an altar.*

2.5 Jars made in this special shape were used as containers for the olive oil given as a prize to the victors in the games celebrating the Great Panathenaia. The inscription says '(One) of the prizes from Athens'. Artists went on painting the warlike Athena on one side and the competition on the other in black on vases of this type long after the style on other vases had changed.

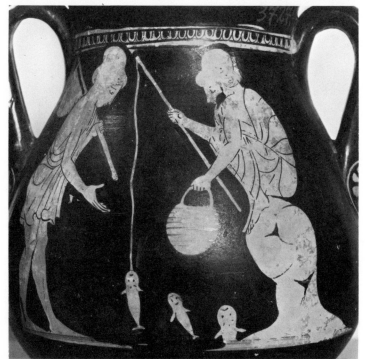

2.4 This Athenian storage jar of the early fifth century BC shows two fishermen. Salted fish played a larger part in the Greek diet than meat, but it was not an everyday food.

of the peplos to an ancient wooden statue of Athena and the sacrifice of many animals in honour of the goddess.

The prizes for the athletic victors were jars of olive oil. The oil came from the olive trees sacred to Athena, all of which were thought to have been grown from cuttings of that first olive tree which Athena produced on the acropolis. Special jars were made to contain the oil, with a picture of Athena on one side and the other side showing the event in which the victor had triumphed (2.5). The first prize could consist of as many as 140 such jars.

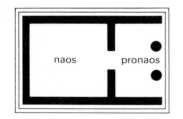

2.6 Plan of a simple temple with a porch at the front. This was the most popular type of temple, of which remains are found all over Greece.

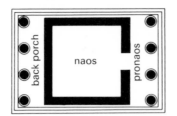

2.8 Plan of a temple with porches in front and at the back.

2.7 This is what such a simple temple would have looked like. In fact, this building (from the early fifth century BC) is not a temple, but a treasury, the treasury of the Athenians at Delphi. Although the type of temple was very popular, few remain standing.

2.9 View of the side of a temple built with porches in front and at the back. It is the temple of Athena Nike in Athens, built in the late fifth century BC.

Temple plans: four basic types

Although nothing more than an altar was really necessary for religious ceremonies, the Greeks sometimes felt that the god or goddess that they worshipped should have a house in which the statue of the divinity could be kept safe from the weather and the birds. It did not have to be very elaborate; a single room was quite enough, with a porch added in front for dignity (2.6). The room was called the *naos* and the porch in front was called the *pronaos* (*pro* is the Greek prefix meaning 'in front of'). This was the simplest kind of temple that the Greeks built (2.7).

Since the Greeks liked things to look balanced, they would often add a porch at the back as well (2.8). The porch did not lead anywhere. It was just for decoration (2.9). When a temple had a porch in front and a porch at the back, its two

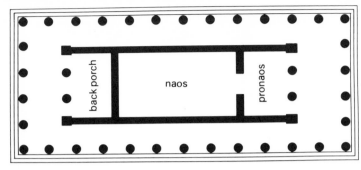

2.10 Plan of the most usual type of peripteral temple.

2.11 View from the corner of a peripteral temple. It is the Hephaisteion in Athens, built around the same time as the Parthenon.

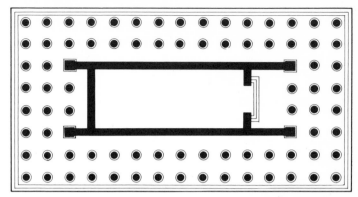

2.12 Plan of a dipteral temple. You can see how complex the plan has become, but you can still recognize the fundamental parts (the naos, pronaos and back porch) and can see how one colonnade has simply surrounded another.

2.13 An artist's reconstruction of what the dipteral temple of Artemis at Ephesus (late fourth century BC) would have looked like. The plan was an enriched version of the simple dipteral plan.

ends looked much the same, but the two sides looked very different from them.

Generally, the Greeks thought a temple would look best if it had the same kind of decoration on all four sides, and so, if they had enough money, they would erect a ring of columns all around the basic core of the temple, that is, a colonnade to surround the naos and its two porches (2.10 and 2.11). The colonnade running around the four sides of the temple is called a *peristyle* (from *peri* – around, and *stylos* – column) and a temple with a peristyle is called *peripteral*. The number of columns along the sides could be anything from eleven to eighteen, but there were usually just six columns along the front and back.

Some very rich cities (these were mostly Ionian cities in or near Asia Minor) built especially grand temples with double peristyles (2.12 and 2.13). These are called *dipteral* temples. They usually had eight columns along the front. You can see why if you compare the plan of the peripteral temple (2.10) with the plan of the dipteral temple (2.12).

13

Temples, you remember, were built to protect the statue of the god, not to accommodate religious rituals or house crowds of worshippers. The ceremonies all took place *outside*, at altars placed to the east of the temple. It was here that the animals were sacrificed and the prayers recited in honour of the god or goddess. The statue of the divinity looking out of the door at the east end of the temple would be well situated to watch the ceremonies. The worshippers standing around the altar would have a good chance to admire the temple.

Temple design: the Doric and Ionic orders

You may have noticed that the columns of the temples and the horizontal beams they hold up can be made in two different ways. On the simplest type of temple (2.7) and the peripteral one (2.11) the columns are stocky, with very simple tops (*capitals*), and above the plain stone band of blocks which they support is another band decorated with alternating striped and unstriped rectangles. In contrast, the temple with two porches (2.9) and the dipteral temple (2.13) have columns that are slender, with more elaborate capitals and quite a different arrangement of the decoration of the upper part.

These are, in fact, two examples of each of the two decorative systems that were used for Greek temples. They are called the Doric order (2.7 and 2.11) and the Ionic order (2.9 and 2.13). Most large temples on mainland Greece were peripteral and built in the Doric order. In and around Asia Minor (Ionia) huge, elaborate dipteral temples were built in the Ionic order.

The Doric order made use of rather sturdy columns – their height was between four and six times their diameter (2.14). The columns rested directly on the top step of the temple.

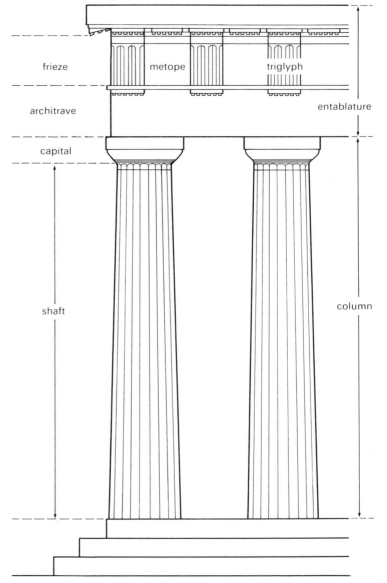

2.14 Corner of a temple in the Doric order.

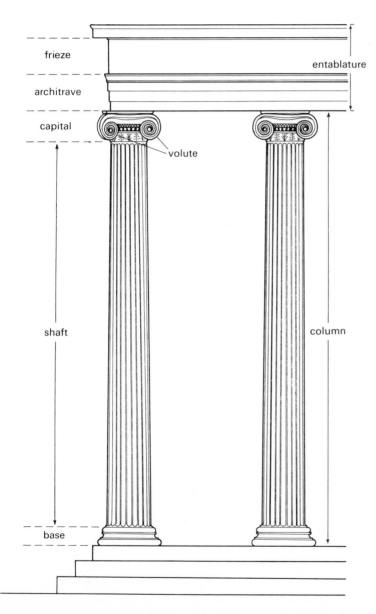

frieze

entablature

architrave

capital

volute

shaft

column

base

(Temples were usually built on three steps.) The columns were topped by capitals that looked like simple cushions and supported a plain horizontal band of stone called an *architrave*. This in turn supported another band, called the *frieze*. The Doric frieze was divided into alternating *triglyphs* (vertically grooved rectangles that remind one of beam ends) and *metopes* (rectangles that could be decorated with paint or sculpture). There was one triglyph over each column and one between each pair. This gave a pleasing visual effect as it repeated, in 'double time', the steady march of the columns below.

The Ionic order made use of slimmer columns – eight to ten times their diameter in height – which rested on a base and were topped by volute capitals (2.15). Above the capitals the architrave was divided into three horizontal steps: a subtle reflection of the three steps below, on which the temple rested. The frieze above was undivided, generally decorated either by a continuous band of relief carvings (2.9) or with the lively regular rhythm of small tooth-like features called *dentils* (2.13).

You have probably noticed on the photographs and drawings that vertical channels or grooves were cut in both Doric and Ionic columns. These are called *flutes*. They are of no importance for the structure of the building and neither strengthen nor weaken the columns, but the Greeks must have thought that they greatly enhanced the beauty of the temple because they take a long time to make and require a great deal of skill.

The fluting on Doric and Ionic columns is different. There are twenty flutes on a Doric column and they meet in a sharp edge. There are twenty-four flutes on an Ionic column, and a smooth band separates each flute from its neighbour.

2.15 Corner of a temple in the Ionic order.

15

2.16 The structural system used for building Greek temples.

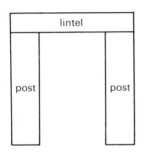

2.17 Section of a Greek temple showing how the roof is supported.

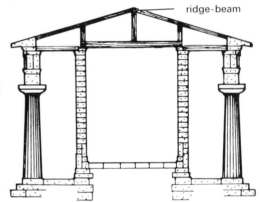

Structural principles

The structural principle used for building a Greek temple is very simple. It is exactly what it appears to be, a *post and lintel* system (2.16). Upright *posts* (or columns or walls) support horizontal *lintels* (beams, architraves or ceilings).

Only the sloping roof is a bit more complicated. The ridge-beam is held up easily enough by vertical supports (2.17); the trick is to make the slope of the rafters so gentle that the tiles on top are kept in place by their own weight (2.18). The pitched roof of a Greek temple, as you can see, leaves a triangular gable (*pediment*) at the front and back which could be filled with sculpture, though it was a difficult task to design sculpture to fit such an awkward space.

Now we are ready to appreciate how a particular temple, the Parthenon, was built.

2.18 The position of the tiles on the gently sloping rafters.

3 Building the Parthenon

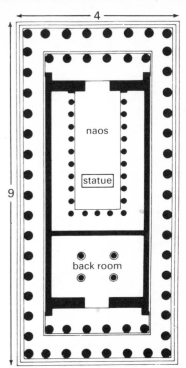

Planning

Before construction could begin on a peripteral Doric temple such as the Parthenon, the architect had to make three major decisions: how long and wide it would be; how many columns it would have in front and along its sides; and, finally, how tall and thick the columns should be.

The architects of the Parthenon decided that its stylobate should be (in modern units) 30.88 metres (101 feet 4 inches) wide and 69.50 metres (228 feet 1 inch) long. The *stylobate* is the top step of the temple, the platform on which the columns stand. There were to be eight columns along the front (not the usual six) and seventeen along the sides. The diameter of the columns was to be 1.91 metres (6 feet 3 inches) where they rested on the stylobate (like all Greek columns, they tapered slightly toward the top) and they were to be 10.43 metres (34 feet 3 inches) high. Unusually, the naos was divided into two parts. The longer eastern section housed the statue of Athena, as might be expected, but the back room, accessible only from the western porch, was something that only rarely appeared in a Greek temple (3.1).

All these decisions must have been approved by the epistatai and ultimately by the Athenian Assembly.

The dimensions of the Parthenon were selected with care and led to subtle relationships between the parts of the temple (3.1). The length of the temple is rather more than twice the width; they are in a ratio of 9:4. It is a ratio worth remembering.

The distance between the columns (measured from axis to axis) is a little more than twice the diameter of the columns (3.2); in fact the ratio of this distance (the *interaxial*) to each diameter is again precisely 9:4.

If you imagine the front of the Parthenon without the pediment and the steps, the front of the temple is a rectangle – whose width to height ratio is once more exactly 9:4.

right: *3.1 Plan of the Parthenon.*

below: *3.2 Elevation of the Parthenon showing the 9:4 ratio of the width to the height and of the interaxial to the diameter of the columns.*

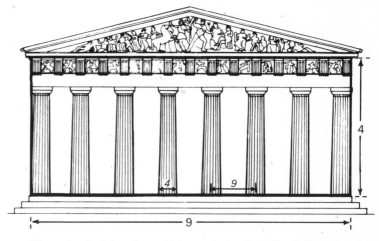

Thus the height, the width, and the length of the temple (and even the relationship of the columns to the spaces between them) are linked in proportions of 9:4.

The whole building, though built in a simple way out of simple parts, has a coherence and harmony that is rooted in mathematics.

17

3.3 Schematic view of the position of the Parthenon seen from the west. Notice the steeply falling south side of the acropolis (to the right) and how it is buttressed.

3.4 A photograph of the south side of the foundations for the Parthenon and its predecessor shows the many courses of regular blocks of limestone that were used to build a solid substructure. Such very deep and solid foundations were not usually provided for Greek temples, but were necessary here because of the position chosen for the temple.

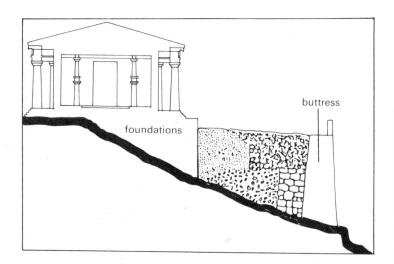

foundations

buttress

Preparing the ground

You will remember that shortly after the battle of Marathon in 490 BC, the Athenians had decided to commemorate their victory by building a grand new temple to Athena on the south side of the acropolis. Except for the bottom step, it was to be constructed entirely out of marble.

Before work on the temple proper could start, parts of the acropolis had to be levelled down and even larger parts had to be built up, especially on the steeply falling south side (3.3). A large solid substructure composed of regular blocks of limestone was erected (3.4).

A great deal of marble had already been quarried and delivered to the acropolis, and the building had made considerable progress before the second Persian invasion in 480 BC put an end to the project. Construction had gone so far that even now it is possible to puzzle out what the plan of the temple was to be (3.5).

3.5 The plan of the temple that the Athenians started to build just after the battle of Marathon is drawn here in black. The plan of the Parthenon, built a generation later, is shown with broken lines.

3.6 Substructure of the Parthenon seen from the west, northern corner. The old foundations are shaded. You can see how they were extended to the north (left) for the Parthenon.

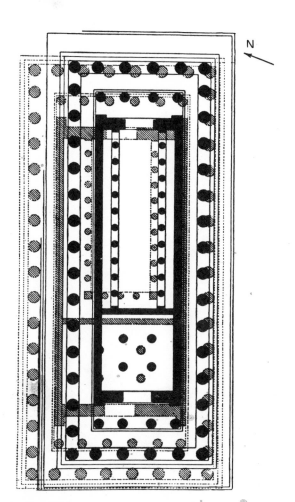

N

The photograph (3.6) shows where the foundations were extended on the north to support the Parthenon. Above the foundations the whole temple, including all three steps it rested on, was built of marble.

Quarrying and transport

The marble came from the quarries on Mount Pentelicon about 16 kilometres (10 miles) from Athens. The Athenians started to make extensive use of the Pentelic quarries only in the fifth century BC. Before that they had imported most of their marble from the island of Paros. Transport of marble was extremely costly, so it had to be used very sparingly for sculptures and architectural trimmings. Had the Pentelic quarries not been close by, the Athenians could never have contemplated so expensive a project as building an entire temple in marble. Close though the quarries were, economies still had to be practised: no more stone was moved than was strictly necessary.

When, a generation later, Pericles proposed building the Parthenon, the same foundations were used since they were on so generous a scale that they had to be extended only slightly to fit the new plan. Notice that the new temple was to have eight columns along the front and back instead of the more usual six planned for the earlier temple.

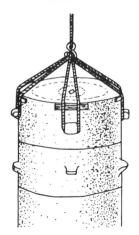

left: *3.7 Column drum as delivered from the quarry.*

right: *3.8 Lifting column drums into position.*

below: *3.9 Bringing marble down from the quarries on sledges.*

Each block of marble was cut from the quarry to the size that was required for its place in the building. The quarrymen hollowed out grooves vertically and horizontally according to the specifications of the architects. They then forced dry wooden wedges into the grooves. The swelling of the wedges when they were wetted split the marble. Blocks quarried for use in columns were trimmed into discs with only four bosses left sticking out where the corners had been (3.7). The bosses were to be used when the discs (column drums) were lifted into position (3.8). Cutting the blocks to size and trimming them before they left the quarry ensured that no unnecessary weight had to be transported.

The blocks of marble were brought down from the quarries on carefully controlled sledges (3.9) along slipways that can still be seen today.

They were then transported to Athens in waggons drawn by oxen. Sometimes as many as thirty or forty yoke of oxen had to be used and the trip may have taken as long as two days.

After it had reached Athens the marble had to be carried up the steep slopes of the acropolis; this time, mules were used to pull the waggons. It must have been hard work and the hearts of the Athenians were touched by the labour of their animals, for they freed those mules that had worked the hardest and let them graze wherever they wished. One mule was supposed to have distinguished himself by coming back of his own free will to offer his services and running along beside the teams that drew the waggons up to the acropolis as if to encourage them.

Setting up the peristyle

The first part of the temple to be erected on the stylobate was the peristyle.

Each column was composed of about ten to twelve drums. The horizontal joins of the drums were divided into four concentric circles and treated in the following manner: the outermost ring was made accurately flat and carefully smoothed for a tight fit; the next ring was cut to the same level,

3.10 The horizontal joins between column drums and the devices for centring.

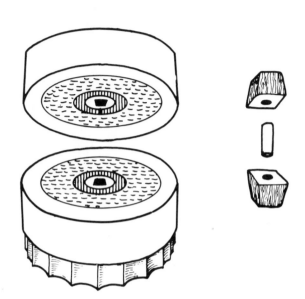

3.11 The ruined drums intended for the temple the Athenians started just after the battle of Marathon were built into the acropolis wall. Notice the fluting at the very bottom of a right-hand drum. It was intended as the lowest drum of a column.

but was slightly roughened to provide a good grip. The third ring was not intended to make close contact with the drum above and was finished less evenly, slightly below the level of the outer rings (in order to save labour). At the centre the surface was again carefully smoothed on a level with the outermost ring. A square plug with a pin in the middle was used to help with centring each drum above the bottom one (3.10). The bottom drum simply rested on the stylobate where its position had been marked.

The fluting of the columns was left until the temple was almost completed, when there was no longer any danger of damaging the delicate flutes in the course of building. The bottom few centimetres of the lowest drum, however, were fluted before they were placed on the stylobate (3.11). This was to prevent any accidental chipping of the finished stylobate when the time came for fluting.

The plan and its key (3.12) show an early stage in the construction of the Parthenon. Notice that the peristyle was nearly complete before the walls of the naos were built up.

3.12 Plan of the Parthenon at an early stage of construction.

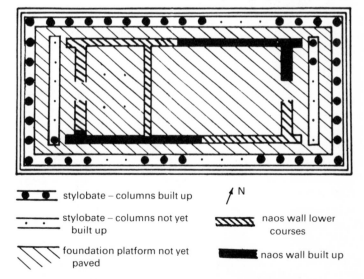

●━● stylobate – columns built up

─── stylobate – columns not yet
∙ ∙ ∙ built up

⧄ foundation platform not yet
paved

↗ N

▨ naos wall lower
courses

▬ naos wall built up

21

3.13 Incomplete temple
at Segesta showing the
stage in building when
no more than the
peristyle has been
erected.

The Doric temple at Segesta in Sicily was never finished. From it you can see what a temple looked like when just the peristyle had been completed (3.13). Notice the unfluted columns, the lifting bosses still in place on the steps and the pavement, and the incomplete stylobate (3.13 and 3.14). It looks as if there are bases under the columns, but in fact this is just the only part of the stylobate that has been laid – the rest would have been inserted when there was less danger of damage during the rest of the building process.

Building the walls

By the fifth century BC the Athenians had become skilled with pulleys, winches and cranes. They were careful to use marble blocks that were small enough to be manoeuvred by such devices.

There were apparently several kinds of pulley (supported on one, two, three or four legs), which could be used as needed to lift column drums and set wall blocks on top of each other (3.15). The four-legged type was used for lifting the greatest weights and could also serve as scaffolding.

The blocks for the walls were laid without mortar. The horizontal surfaces were so carefully smoothed that they fitted perfectly and the joins are practically invisible, even if viewed from near by. The vertical ends of adjoining blocks were hollowed out slightly at the centre and bottom, leaving a smooth edge only at the top and sides to make a close fit. This treatment of the ends of the blocks is called *anathyrosis* and

3.14 The steps of the base and parts of the stylobate of the incomplete temple at Segesta, showing the lifting bosses still in place. Unusually the very bottom of the lowest drums of the columns have not been fluted. Had they got around to fluting the columns, the masons would probably have been very sorry that they had omitted to take this precaution.

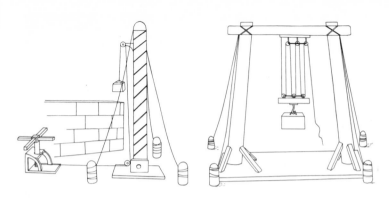
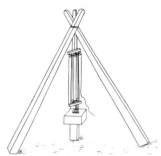
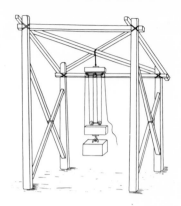

above: *3.15 Different types of pulleys and cranes used by the Athenians. Their experience as sailors must have helped them to design and manipulate these devices.*

below: *3.16 Workmen levering wall blocks into position. Notice the anathyrosis and the double 'T' clamps. These iron clamps, which were used to hold neighbouring blocks together, were totally encased in lead in order to prevent rusting. Similar methods were used to attach blocks vertically.*

means 'like the frame of a door' (3.16). It must have been a relief to the workmen that they could leave the sunken portion just roughed out and did not have to work the whole surface so meticulously.

Each row of blocks was level. Two teams of workmen would often start laying a course from each end of the wall. Holes were cut in the blocks to help the men lever them into position. Metal clamps in the shape of a double 'T' were used to hold neighbouring blocks together (3.16).

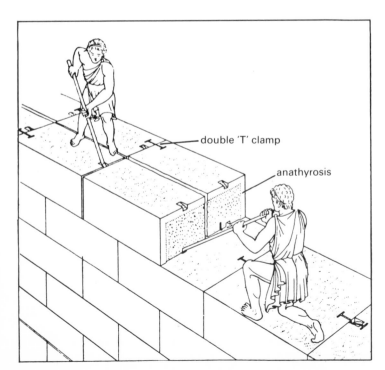

double 'T' clamp

anathyrosis

3.17 The device used for levelling looked like a capital letter 'A'. A plumb line hung from its apex. When this coincided with the vertical line cut on the cross bar, masons could be sure that the two surfaces they were measuring were level. What might the other architectural implements represented on this Roman relief have been used for?

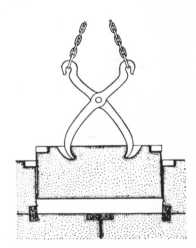

3.18 The last block in a row would come somewhere in the centre and would have to be lowered into position by tongs.

23

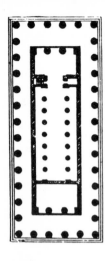

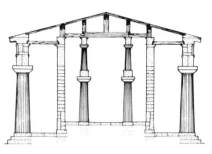

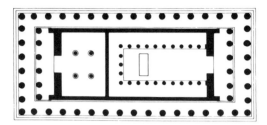

3.22 Plan of the Parthenon. The four columns in the back room were Ionic and stood on bases, as is indicated on the plan.

3.19 Plan of the second temple of Hera at Paestum in Italy showing the usual two rows of internal columns. The temple was built around 460 BC.

above: 3.20 Section of the same temple showing the double-tiered inner colonnades.

The interior

The Greeks were afraid their timbers were not strong enough to reach from wall to wall to provide a ceiling for the naos and a support for the roof. They therefore tried to find a way to reduce the space to be covered. They did this by means of two rows of columns which ran from the front to the back of the naos parallel to the walls (3.19).

Doric columns like those of the peristyle would have taken up a lot of room and would have made the naos unbearably crowded. So the Greeks made the interior colonnades double-tiered (3.20). Doric columns that were shorter than the peristyle columns would also be narrower and so take up less floor space. The columns above, being still shorter, would have even smaller diameters (3.21).

Most Doric peripteral temples had only six columns along the front and back. The Parthenon had eight because Phidias wanted to have an exceptionally broad naos so that he could show off the magnificent statue of Athena that he was making. The statue was the most important part of the entire project; it cost almost twice as much as the rest of the temple put together and Phidias as its sculptor had a considerable say in the temple's design.

Instead of just running the columns down the two sides of the naos, Phidias also put some round the back (3.22 and 3.23), thus producing a 'U'-shaped space to set off his statue.

The small back room of the Parthenon presented another problem. Only four columns (3.22) were required to hold up the ceiling and they would have looked odd double-tiered. The architects' solution was to use Ionic columns. These were slenderer than Doric and so could reach the desired height while taking up less floor space.

These four Ionic columns constitute one of several Ionic features in the Doric Parthenon.

3.21 The double-tiered inner colonnades of the second temple of Hera at Paestum.

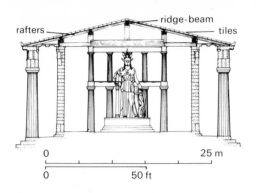

left: *3.23
Section of the
Parthenon
showing how
the roof was
supported.*

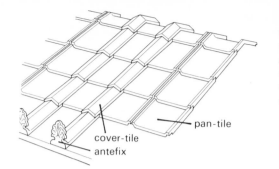

left: *3.24
Pan-tiles and
cover-tiles.
Antefixes are
attached at the
ends of the
cover-tiles.*

⟨Roofing⟩

Huge wooden beams and rafters supported the roof of the Parthenon. The roof tiles rested on a bedding laid over the rafters (3.23).

There were two kinds of tile: flat pan-tiles with raised edges placed one beside the other and ridged cover-tiles that bridged the joins between the pan-tiles and made the roof watertight (3.24).

Normally, the ends of the final cover-tiles were ornamented with decorative attachments (in the shape of heads or floral palmettes) called *antefixes* (3.24). These livened up the otherwise dull line at the bottom of the roof along the side of the temple.

Most roof tiles were made of terracotta shaped in moulds, but the tiles of the Parthenon were expensively cut from imported Parian marble.

As the Parthenon was a large temple, the antefixes had to be fairly widely spaced along its sides if they were to look handsome. The nature of marble set practical limits to the size of the pan-tiles: if they were thin and broad the marble was in danger of cracking; if they were made thicker the weight would be too great to be supported. Thus they had to be relatively small, and it was not possible to make the positions of the antefixes and the cover-tiles coincide. The architects therefore decided that every second antefix should mask the end of a line of large cover-tiles in the usual way, but the intermediate antefixes should just be centred between two lines of smaller cover-tiles (3.25).

Finally six *acroteria* (decorations attached above the three angles of the pediment) were placed at the four corners of the roof and at the top of each gable (3.26). Sometimes the

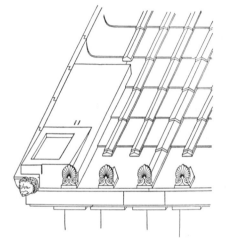

left: *3.25 The
arrangement of roof
tiles and antefixes on
the Parthenon.*

below: *3.26
Reconstruction
drawing of the
completed Parthenon
showing the
placement of the
acroteria and the
antefixes.*

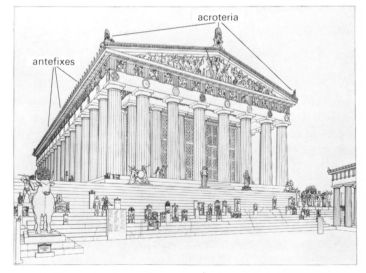

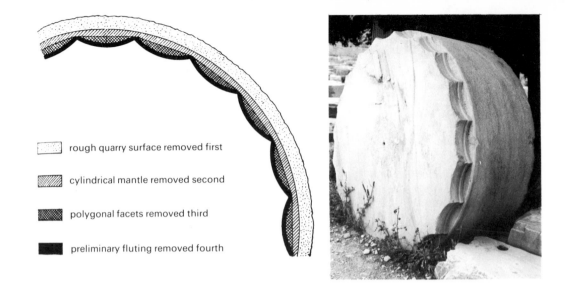

right: *3.27 Diagram showing the four stages in fluting a column.*

far right: *3.28 Photograph of an unfinished column drum showing two stages in cutting back from the cylindrical mantle.*

☐ rough quarry surface removed first

▨ cylindrical mantle removed second

▧ polygonal facets removed third

■ preliminary fluting removed fourth

acroteria that crowned temples were representations of sphinxes or winged figures or even groups of figures, but on the Parthenon they were huge, symmetrical floral designs. In fact the rather free plant forms of the acroteria were meant to lessen the severity of the triangular ends of the roof of the temple, just as the antefixes were supposed to soften the harsh lines of the sides.

Finishing

Once all the structural work had been completed and the temple had been roofed, the time came for finishing. This was a painstaking job, executed with the utmost care. All the bosses that had been left protruding from blocks and columns were chiseled off and all the surfaces of the temple, which until then had been left with a thin layer of stone for protection, were worked back to their final intended level and made perfectly smooth.

Now at last the columns were fluted, a job that was done in no less than four consecutive stages (3.27 and 3.28).

The beauty of the Parthenon depended not only on the precision of the construction but also on the perfection of the finishing, the smooth surfaces of walls and columns, the virtual invisibility of joins, and the knife-edge clarity of the fluting.

Refinements

Most of what has been said so far could describe the way almost any Doric peripteral temple was built. But the Parthenon was unusual. It was unusual not only in the exquisite care that was taken in the actual carving and finishing of all its parts, but also in the subtleties that were built into its design and the abundance of sculpture with which it was decorated.

Before we turn to the sculpture, at least three of the so-called *architectural refinements* should be mentioned (3.29).

The first has to do with all the horizontals in the building. On all four sides of the Parthenon there was a slight upward curvature towards the centre. Some people think this was done to prevent the middle of each side of the temple from appearing to sag; others think it was done simply to enliven the appearance of a building which might otherwise look too regular; some, prosaically, think it was just for drainage. What is remarkable is that the curvature of the base, which starts at the foundations, is carried right up through the entablature.

The second refinement has to do with the tapering of the columns. The columns do not taper along a straight line, but have a slight swelling along the line of taper about two-thirds of the way up. This is called *entasis* and was used in earlier temples, but not so subtly as on the Parthenon.

A third refinement concerns the angle at which the columns

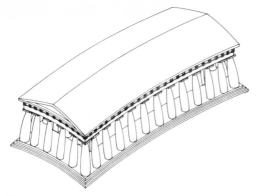

are set. None of the columns is strictly vertical. All the columns lean slightly inward; the corner columns have a double slope.

Any simple post and lintel structure made out of many identical repeated units is in danger of looking lifeless and mechanical. Many buildings that imitate the Parthenon do. The architectural refinements are meant to counteract this. They modify just those parts of the temple that otherwise would look most severe and rigid: the straight lines and right angles. Thus the horizontal lines of the steps and the entablature are slightly arched and even the tapering of the columns is turned into a gentle curve. The slope of the columns avoids the sharpness of a right angle and even the hard-edged lines of the roof are enlivened by the antefixes and acroteria.

The men who built the Parthenon

The Parthenon was built chiefly by men who knew how to work marble.

The quarrymen had to have considerable skill in order to be able to cut blocks to specific measurements straight from the rock face. They also had to know how to avoid the faults, which are numerous in Pentelic marble, that might spoil a fine edge or mar a surface. The architects would reject (and even return to the quarries) any blocks that did not come up to the required standards, for one of the principal functions of the architects was to inspect the marble as it arrived.

The stonemasons also needed particular skills. Foreigners and slaves worked side by side with Athenian citizens, doing the same jobs and receiving the same pay. The quality of their work, not their social status, was what mattered.

A big project like the Parthenon attracted masons from far and wide, who flocked to Athens to offer their services. Temple building was a specialized craft, and there would not be many men throughout Greece capable of practising it. They moved around from place to place, working where they were needed. When, by the end of the fifth century BC, the Athenians were no longer commissioning new public buildings, the craftsmen dispersed, carrying their skill and experience with them to other Greek cities and even beyond the confines of the Greek-speaking world.

The marble was quarried and worked with iron tools: picks, points, punches, chisels and drills (4.22). In most instances the tool was held against the surface of the stone and was firmly hit or gently tapped by a hammer or a mallet.

Men skilled in other crafts were also necessary, particularly those who could work with wood and metal. Carpenters and joiners erected scaffoldings and constructed the wooden ceiling and roof. Metalworkers fashioned the clamps that held the blocks of stone together and took care of the iron tools.

Unskilled labourers also had work. They were needed to load and unload the marble and to move it from place to place on the site. Farmers owning one or two oxen could hire out their own and their animals' services when they were not busy working the land. There were no haulage contractors in the modern sense, and so even rather modest help with transport was not scorned.

Skilled workmen received one drachma a day; unskilled ones less. The architects also received just one drachma a day despite the greater responsibility they carried in planning the work and approving it at every stage. It may be that they were little more than master-masons, but it is also possible that sometimes they were learned and wealthy men who contributed their skill and labour as a kind of public service and received only a token fee.

4 The sculptures of the Parthenon

The position of the sculptures

The Parthenon was unusual in the richness of its decoration. The amount of sculpture that adorned its exterior was un-parallelled in the Greek world.

Pediments were often filled with sculptures. Since the Parthenon had eight columns at its ends (like an Ionic dipteral temple) the space for pedimental sculptures was abnormally wide and it contained very many extremely large figures. These were carved fully in the round as if they were free-standing statues.

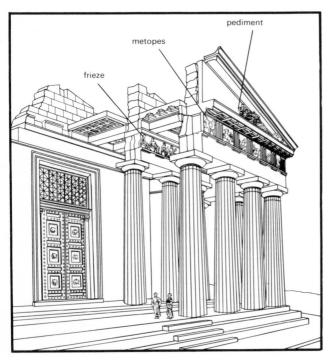

4.1 Diagram showing the position of the sculptures on the Parthenon.

Many Doric buildings had carved metopes. Only if the building was small, like the tiny treasury of the Athenians, built at Delphi after the battle of Marathon (2.7), was it likely that metopes on all four sides would be carved; most larger buildings had only a few metopes sculpted. On the Parthenon, however, all ninety-two metopes were decorated with sculptures carved in high relief.

Normally, a Doric temple would have no continuous frieze. Not so the Parthenon. The frieze, carved in low relief, not only decorated the area over the porches (4.1), but also ran along the top of the side walls of the naos. Like the eight columns in front and at the back, the frieze was an unexpected Ionic touch introduced into a mainly Doric building.

The sculptures were all placed high up on the temple, but they were made easier to understand at a distance by the addition of colour which picked out hair, eyes and clothing, and helped the figures to stand out against a painted background. Pieces of bronze were attached to the stone to indicate the bridles and reins of horses and other such details.

The metopes 447–442 BC

The sculptures adorning the Parthenon were more than mere decoration. They all had a meaning. The carved metopes, for instance, portrayed mythical battles – a different one on each side. Those on the south side showed the conflict of the Lapiths (legendary men who were supposed to have lived in northern Greece) with the centaurs (monsters who were part man and part horse).

The story was that the Lapiths were neighbours of the centaurs and when the Lapith king got married, he invited the centaurs to the wedding as a matter of common courtesy. At first all went well, but after a while the centaurs got drunk and misbehaved, attacking the women and breaking the place up (4.2). After a violent fight, the Lapiths beat the centaurs and drove them from their country.

4.2 *Painting on a Greek vase, made some time after the Parthenon was finished, illustrating the story of the battle of the Lapiths and centaurs.*

The Greeks often saw myths as examples of human experience. The story of the Lapiths and centaurs would have suggested to them that the centaurs were ill-mannered brutes and the Lapiths who defeated them were civilized and brave. They would have wondered if this story could in some way apply to their own lives or recent history. 'The centaurs', they might have thought, 'in their wild and barbaric actions behaved very much like the Persians who so rudely invaded us, their neighbours.' The Lapiths' victory over the centaurs would then seem to them like a mythological parallel to the Greeks' recent victory over the Persians.

The other stories illustrated in the metopes (Amazons attacking Athenians, gods fighting giants, and the Trojan war) could also, with a little thought, be seen in this light, as mythical allegories of the Persian wars.

Once the subjects had been selected, sculptors had to be found to carve the representations, and this was a matter of some urgency. The metopes had to be ready to be slipped into place once the peristyle had been erected, so that work could continue above them. They seem to have been in position by 442 BC.

The carving of ninety-two metopes, each about 1.3 metres (4 feet 3 inches) square, in something under five years was no small undertaking, and sculptors were hurriedly collected from all over Greece. Some were better than others. There was no time to train them all to reach the same standards or the same artistic ideals.

4.3 *The centaur's face in metope 31 from the south side of the Parthenon is almost a caricature.*

4.4 *By contrast, the centaur in metope 30 from the south side of the Parthenon is portrayed with a humane and compassionate face.*

29

left: *4.5 Metope 8 from the south side of the Parthenon. The centaur has forced a Lapith down so that he is squatting on his heel. His position is like that of the Lapith in metope 30 (4.4 on page 29), but the way his leg is carved is very different.*

The sculptors differed markedly from one another in their interpretations of the story. One sculptor carved a centaur with a crude and barbaric face, almost like a mask (4.3), while another portrayed a centaur with so kindly an expression that he could be imagined as a loving grandfather (4.4).

The sculptors also differed in their ability and the quality of their carvings. The 'grandfatherly' centaur has forced the Lapith down so that he is sitting on one heel. Look carefully at the leg that is bent under the Lapith. Now look at the leg of another Lapith who has been forced into a similar position (4.5). The first Lapith's leg looks rather like a folded sausage, while the other is carved to show the contrast between straining muscles and soft, yielding flesh.

Some of the sculptors were superb.

One of the best of them worked on the metope at the far western end of the south side of the Parthenon (4.6). This metope is both beautifully designed and beautifully executed. Since it is still in place on the building, one can appreciate the wonderful animation that is given to the figures by the brilliant Athenian sunlight, and the vitality and humanity that these sculptures impart to the architecture.

4.6 Metope 1 still in place on the south side of the Parthenon at the west end. The other three metopes illustrated here showing the combat of Lapiths and centaurs were removed from the building by Lord Elgin in 1801 and are now in the British Museum in London.

4.7 View of the external frieze and the frieze over the porch on a normal Doric temple. Notice that both friezes are divided into triglyphs and metopes. This is the so-called temple of Concord at Agrigento in Sicily, built about the same time as the Parthenon.

4.8 View of the external frieze and the frieze over the west porch on the Parthenon.

The frieze 442—438 BC

The frieze was the next part of the architectural sculpture to be completed.

In a normal Doric temple you would see triglyphs and metopes above the columns of the porch (4.7). What a surprise to look up inside the peristyle of the Parthenon (4.8)!

It is worth remembering that the frieze could in fact be seen only through the screen of the columns of the peristyle, an important point for the designer.

The design of the frieze was a great challenge. It was an immensely long ribbon, a mere 1 metre (3 feet 3 inches) high and almost 160 metres (525 feet) long. The theme chosen for the frieze was a procession, forming up in the west porch and

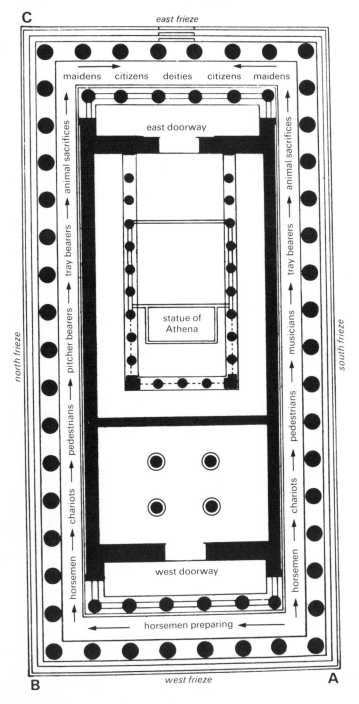

east frieze

maidens citizens deities citizens maidens

east doorway

animal sacrifices

animal sacrifices

tray bearers

tray bearers

north frieze

south frieze

pitcher bearers

musicians

statue of
Athena

pedestrians

pedestrians

chariots

chariots

horsemen

horsemen

west doorway

horsemen preparing

B

A

west frieze

left: *4.9 Plan of the Parthenon with the order of the procession on the frieze described upon it.*

below: *4.10 View of the Parthenon from the northwest, as it is seen on entering the acropolis.*

proceeding along both the north and south sides of the temple towards the east, where its two branches converged (4.9). This was the front of the temple.

In the plan, the direction of the procession seems to change rather abruptly at the southwest corner (A), which might be expected to give an awkward visual effect, but in fact it was very carefully calculated in terms of how a visitor would actually approach the Parthenon. The visitor first saw the Parthenon from the northwest corner (B) (4.10); the whole west side could be taken in at a glance (A–B). He would normally walk along the north side to the front of the temple (B–C), keeping pace with the sculpted procession. There was little temptation to walk along the south, since the space between the temple and the edge of the acropolis (from which there was a sheer drop) was narrow.

4.11 Part of the representation of a chariot in full gallop from the south side of the Parthenon frieze, now in the British Museum in London. The man, wearing a helmet and carrying a shield, was one of the 'apobatai', men who performed the daring feat of jumping on and off swiftly moving chariots. This exercise of skill was part of the display that accompanied the celebration of the Great Panathenaia.

Visual logic rather than abstract theory dictated the design of the frieze.

The procession included a large number of horsemen (4.8), some men in chariots (4.11), and youths carrying trays or water jars (4.17) or conducting animals to sacrifice. At the east, moving very slowly, girls with offering bowls converged on an assembly of gods (4.15) and heroes. In the very centre an official and his assistant are handling a large folded cloth, perhaps the peplos for the statue of Athena (4.12).

The procession must have reminded the Athenians of the Great Panathenaic procession in honour of Athena, which regularly moved side by side with the sculpted frieze. It is unlikely, however, that the decoration of a temple at this time would merely represent a common event in the lives of ordinary people.

No surviving ancient account so much as mentions the frieze, so it is up to modern scholars to ponder what it might have meant. The most appealing suggestion is that the frieze represents the last celebration of the Great Panathenaia in which the men who later died at Marathon participated. Within two months of the festival they gave their lives to preserve Athena's city. An ingenious counting of the men portrayed (excluding the charioteers but including unmounted youths) arrives at the number 192, the very number of those who fell at Marathon. According to this theory the gods are assembled to receive the heroic dead into the realm of immortal fame. This could explain why they all turn their attention towards the approaching processions while seeming to ignore the central scene with the peplos.

The solemnity of the procession and the unique honours that were accorded to the men who died at Marathon support this interpretation. You remember that the Parthenon itself had a special connection with Marathon, for it stood on the site of a building that had been begun just after the battle to commemorate the victory.

The idea of a sculpted procession accompanying the route of a real one has no parallel in Greece, but it has in Persia. There, in the great palace at Persepolis built between 500 and 460 BC, processions were carved to line the stairways and passages traversed by the participants in the traditional annual tribute-bearing processions (4.16).

Since the time of the Persian wars Athenian ambassadors and many other famous Greeks had visited Persia. Furthermore the sculptors who worked at Persepolis, under Persian orders and in Persian style, were Greeks. Reports of the great friezes at Persepolis had certainly reached the Athenians. Could their own unprecedented frieze on the Parthenon have been an artistic and ideological reply to the creation of their old enemy?

33

4.12 The central portion of the east frieze of the Parthenon.
In the centre, a woman, perhaps the priestess of Athena, turns towards two girls carrying something on their heads. Back to back with her is an official who is folding a large piece of cloth, perhaps the peplos, with the help of a little girl. The gods sit on either side, their backs turned to the central scene.

The gods are shown as larger than the human beings; although they are seated, their heads are on the same level as those of the standing adults. The gods are (from left to right): Iris (the attendant of Hera), Hera (the wife of Zeus), Zeus. On the right side of the central scene is Athena, chatting to her brother, the craftsman god, Hephaistos. He helped with her unusual birth, the story of which is illustrated in the east pediment of the Parthenon.

This long slab of carving was found built into a wall on the acropolis and on Lord Elgin's orders was brought to England. In the process of shipping, it cracked in the middle.

The screen of columns behind which the frieze was seen was used on the north and the south sides, and to some extent on the west (4.8) as a foil to the movement of the procession: the steady, even march of the columns contrasting with the spurts of activity and the solemn slowing down of horses, chariots, and men on foot. On the east, the front of the temple, the columns framed significant or striking groups. Thus between the central columns was seen the ritual with the peplos flanked by the most important gods: Zeus with his wife Hera on the left, and Athena herself with the craftsman god Hephaistos – the two great patrons of Athenian prosperity – on the right (4.13 and 4.12).

4.13 This drawing shows how the central slab from the east frieze of the Parthenon would have appeared between the columns of the peristyle to someone standing on the ground in front of the temple looking up at its decoration.

What makes people think the sculpture is so beautiful?

Phidias, the director of works and sculptor of the statue inside the temple, was probably also in charge of the sculptures decorating the outside. By the time the frieze was carved he had succeeded in impressing his ideas on the many sculptors he had gathered together and who had worked on the metopes. The carving of the frieze is generally of higher quality and the style is more uniform than on the metopes. For all that, you may still be wondering why these sculptures, battered as they are, having lost all their colours and very often their heads and arms as well, are so admired. Two examples may suggest the reasons.

4.14 Three gods sculpted in low relief, from the frieze of the Siphnian Treasury in Delphi carved around 525 BC.

First, look at the seated gods that were carved around 525 BC for a small frieze at Delphi (4.14). They are very charming, and represent some of the finest work done by Greek sculptors in the century before the Parthenon was built. Notice how the poses of the figures are repeated and how the raised arms of the two at the left produce a repeated rhythm. Notice the delightful identical patterns that are used over and over again in the clothing and the hair.

Now look at the three gods sculpted on the Parthenon frieze (4.15). See how natural and relaxed they appear, how casually they seem to sit, how varied are the folds of their clothing and the locks of their hair. It all looks so simple and easy, and yet it has been meticulously thought out. Each figure's pose is carefully distinguished from that of its neighbour. The first sits sideways, nearly in profile, with his head in profile; the next sits in a three-quarter front view with his head in a three-quarter front view; the third sits in a three-quarter front view, too, but with her head in profile. Though differentiated, the figures are also united. Notice, for instance, the lower arms of the three figures: the first drops, the second is lifted halfway up, the third is bent right up – they are like film stills of one continuous movement.

4.15 Three gods carved in low relief, from the east frieze of the Parthenon. The gods are seated right of the centre and so are looking right – towards the procession that is approaching them. They are Poseidon, Apollo and Artemis. This slab is now in the Acropolis Museum in Athens.

below: *4.17 Four youths carrying water jars, from the north side of the Parthenon frieze. The portrayal on the frieze was not intended to be absolutely true to life, for in the real Great Panathenaia girls carried the water. Notice the subtle differences in the positions of the heads and the near arms of the three standing figures. This slab is now in the Acropolis Museum in Athens.*

Or compare the almost contemporary carving of four men in the frieze at Persepolis (4.16) with the four water carriers from the Parthenon frieze (4.17). The carving at Persepolis is very fine, but the figures are a bit dull and repetitive. There is a sameness about them that even affects the shape of the spaces between them. How different are the youths from the Parthenon frieze, each of whom is slightly but perceptibly unlike the others. Notice how different even the spaces between them are.

As we have seen, the Parthenon frieze may have been the Athenians' response to the Persepolis frieze of their former great enemy, Persia. While the Persians show the regimentation of subject peoples paying tribute to a powerful king, the Athenians show the easy self-imposed discipline of free citizens freely offering homage not to a man, but to their goddess.

The pediments 438–432 BC

The pediments were the last part of the sculptured decoration to be finished. They could be carved at leisure on the ground since tackles were used to lift them into place, and the roofing of the temple did not depend on their being in position. Final payment was made for them in 432 BC, so they must have been completed by then. Phidias seems to have left Athens after he finished making the great statue of Athena in 438 BC. It was just at this time that serious work began on the pediments, so that although Phidias may have designed them, their execution must have been largely independent of him.

The west pediment, though at the back of the temple, was the first one that you saw as you approached the Parthenon (4.10). It showed the contest of Athena and Poseidon for the patronage of Athens.

4.18 *A drawing made in 1674 of the west pediment of the Parthenon.*

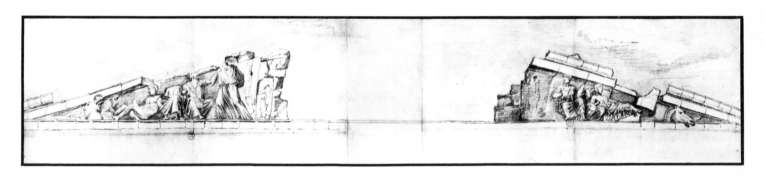

4.19 *A drawing (by the same artist) of the east pediment.*

The east pediment, at the front, showed the astonishing birth of Athena. All the gods and goddesses were gathered for the occasion (just as they were gathered on the east side of the frieze within the porch to celebrate the anniversary of that occasion, Athena's birthday).

Little is left of these two great compositions. A drawing made in the seventeenth century gives some hint of what the west pediment looked like then (4.18), but few of the statues shown have survived. Even by that time the whole centre of the east pediment had already been lost, as you can see from another drawing by the same artist (4.19).

Modern scholars have tried to fill the gap and have made ingenious reconstructions of the centre of the east pediment. Though some efforts look better than others, they are certainly all very far from what the original must have been like.

Some of the statues from near the corners are preserved in the British Museum. Three goddesses, two seated and one lying down so that they will all fit comfortably under the slope of the pediment, give some idea of the quality of the work (4.20). The figures are huge – well over life-size. Their bodies are clothed in loose drapery with many ridges that would catch the light and make the forms beneath clear, even to a viewer standing far below.

The first woman sits facing front, the second turns a little to the side, a third reclines with her upper body turned a little to the side but her legs fully to the side. The progression from full front to full side view is accomplished in stages. The sculptor is working out in three dimensions something rather like the series of continuous movements we observed in the dropped, raised, and bent forearms of the gods on the frieze (4.15).

Look at the back view of these lovely figures (4.21). Notice how differently the pliable cloth falls over the soft rounded bodies and over the hard angular seat. It is remarkable that such exquisite care was lavished on a part of the statues that was never supposed to be seen again once they were put in place.

above: *4.20 Three goddesses from one corner of the east pediment of the Parthenon.*

below: *4.21 Back view of the same three goddesses.*

The celebrated statue of Athena

The abundance and splendour of the sculptures that decorated the outside of the Parthenon may well impress us, but the art-lovers of antiquity seem hardly to have noticed them. Neither the frieze nor the metopes are even mentioned by any Greek or Roman writer whose works we have, and of the pediments no more is said than what their subjects were. All enthusiasm was reserved for the wonderful statue within.

Phidias, who made it, was a great innovator in matters of interpretation, size and technique. His images of gods, lavishly covered in rich materials, were larger and more awe-inspiring than any that had been seen before.

The Athena in the Parthenon was about 10 metres (33 feet) tall; her face and arms and feet were veneered in ivory, her clothing thickly plated in gold, her eyes inset with precious stones. Statues made in this way – Phidias made another one for the temple of Zeus at Olympia – are called *chryselephantine* (gold and ivory). Of course the gold and ivory were only attached to the surface of the statue. The body, head and limbs were constructed on an armature (a sort of internal scaffolding) of wood, the hollow parts of which (according to the wags) provided homes for families of mice.

The only light in the naos came from the door. A visitor stepped out of the brilliant Greek sunshine into a darkened room. At the back of it stood the huge statue of Athena. The gold of her dress glimmered, the ivory of her skin glowed, the gems in her eyes flashed. There was a pool of water in front of the statue (to keep the humidity steady and so prevent the ivory from cracking); it must have caught the light and reflected the statue.

The peplos that was offered to Athena on the occasion of the Great Panathenaia was not used to drape this statue. It was given to a much smaller, age-old image of the goddess made out of olivewood which was kept somewhere on the north side of the acropolis, in any case not in the Parthenon. The ancient, sacred olivewood statue was supposed to have fallen from heaven. It probably did not look very impressive; in fact it may have appeared rather crude. The Athena in the Parthenon was not that sort of holy image of the goddess; it was, rather, a rich thank-offering presented to her.

The statue was a gift to Athena, like an immense jewel; the Parthenon was built to shelter and contain it. No altar for sacrifices was erected in front of the Parthenon. The temple was apparently not thought of as a place of worship, but as a sort of vast jewel box, a necessary part of the offering that was made to the goddess. If that is understood, one can see why the ancient authors took comparatively little notice of its external decoration and turned all their attention to the costly and glorious dedication within.

The wooden core of the statue was easily damaged and we know of many repairs; a major reconstruction may have been necessary as early as the second century BC. By the end of the middle ages all traces of the statue had completely disappeared.

It is difficult to get any idea of what the Athena in the Parthenon actually looked like. We only have some rather long descriptions (they are mostly concerned with details of decoration) and some copies that were made, on a reduced scale, of stone. One of the earliest, largest, and handsomest of these is obviously a very free rendering. More literal copies were made later, some as souvenirs for the Romans, the tourists of antiquity. By and large they are depressingly ugly. They certainly do not convey an impression of what must have been the supreme glory of the Parthenon.

The men who made the sculptures of the Parthenon

Marble sculptors, like the stonemasons who were temple builders, had specialized skills that were only occasionally in demand. They lived itinerant lives, moving wherever work was to be found. Many of them even worked for the Persians at Persepolis (p. 33).

The vast amount of sculpture needed for the decoration of the Parthenon – ninety-two figured metopes, nearly fifty over-life-size pedimental statues, and hundreds of men and animals carved on the frieze – drew sculptors to Athens like a magnet. The diversity of their backgrounds and training can be seen in the differences apparent in the carving of the metopes (4.3 – 4.6). The strong personality of Phidias had welded them together by the time they began working on the frieze. Differences in quality between one part of the frieze and another are not very marked.

The sculptors used iron tools similar to those employed by the stonemasons (4.22). Sometimes sculptors also worked as architects. It is easy to see why. We sometimes hear of families of sculptors. Obviously fathers were eager to pass their skill on to their sons.

A staff of specialists must have assisted Phidias with his work on the gold and ivory statue of Athena. Many of them probably accompanied Phidias when he left Athens to go and make another statue in the same technique at Olympia.

Once the pediments were finished, there was not so much work for marble sculptors to do in Athens. Some worked on the other temples that were being built, others kept busy carving gravestones. Most left, carrying their style and skill with them, diffusing the lessons learned from creating the sculpture of the Parthenon throughout the Greek-speaking world and even beyond.

Phidias' strong personality, his genius as an artist, his friendship with Pericles and his ability as an organizer and director of work may have been very good for the Parthenon, but it did not make his own life easy. When political enemies wished to attack Pericles, they accused his friend Phidias of embezzling some of the gold intended for the statue. The charge was

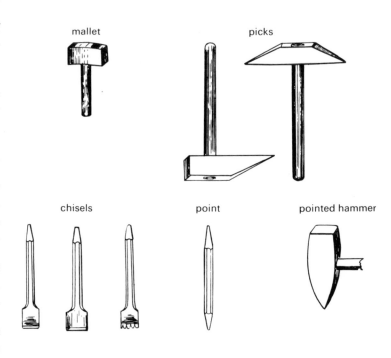

4.22 *Some tools used by stonemasons and sculptors.*

mallet   picks

chisels   point   pointed hammer

disproved, but it is significant that one of Phidias' own workmen had been persuaded to level it at him. Jealousy and discord must have often erupted among the sculptors who had been so hastily assembled. Yet in a mere fifteen years they were able to produce all the harmonious-seeming sculptures that decorated the Parthenon.

5 The Parthenon in the fifth century BC and later

The Parthenon in Periclean Athens

At the time the Parthenon was being built not everybody approved of spending so much public money on such a thing. Political enemies of Pericles accused him of misusing the League funds for his building projects. They reproached him with 'gilding their city and ornamenting it with statues and costly temples, as a proud and vain woman decks herself out in jewels'. Many people must have agreed with them, for when Pericles asked the Assembly of citizens if they thought he was spending too much, they said yes.

'Very well then,' Pericles retorted, 'do not let it be charged to the public account but to my own, and I will dedicate the buildings in my own name.' A great roar went up from the crowd and the people cried out that Pericles might spend as much as he wished on the buildings – from the public treasury.

Pericles' building projects, of which the Parthenon was one, belonged to his vision of what Athens should be. This vision is also expressed in parts of the Funeral Oration he is supposed to have delivered shortly after the Parthenon was completed:

'Our constitution,' he explained, 'is called a democracy because power is not in the hands of a few, but of the people. Our laws secure equal justice for all in their private disputes, and our public opinion welcomes and honours talent in every branch of achievement; what counts is not membership in a particular class, but the actual ability a man possesses.

'Yet ours is no mere work-a-day city. No other provides so much recreation for the spirit – contests and sacrifices all the year round, and beauty in our public buildings to cheer the heart and delight the eye day by day.

'We are lovers of the beautiful without being extravagant, and lovers of wisdom without being soft. We regard wealth as something to be used properly, rather than as something to boast about ... We decide and debate, carefully, and in person, all matters of policy, for we do not think there is an incompatibility between words and deeds.

'Our city,' he concluded, 'is an education to Greece.'

Such was the ideal of Athens that Pericles tried, in different ways, to realize.

By the middle of the fifth century BC Athens' cultural leadership was as obvious as her political ambitions. Gifted individuals of all kinds were drawn to her. Sculptors and stonemasons were attracted for the sake of the work she provided; poets, philosophers, and scientists came for the sake of her rich intellectual life. Though foreigners did not have the rights and privileges of citizens – it was to citizens that Pericles addressed his Funeral Oration – the disadvantages were apparently not enough to discourage them from flocking to the city; they, too, felt it was an education to Greece.

The citizens were proud of Athens' cultural activity. The magnificent buildings and sculptures that were being erected impressed visitors, as did the splendid tragedies and comedies that were performed in the theatre of Dionysus on the south slope of the acropolis in the shadow of the Parthenon (photograph, page 1). Plays by Euripides, whose works were first performed shortly before the Parthenon was begun, were so far famed and so passionately admired that Athenian prisoners of war in distant Sicily in 413 BC could buy their freedom if they were able to recite his latest verses to their captors.

Representatives of the members of the Delian League came to participate in the great festivals of Athens, the Great Panathenaia and the City Dionysia (in which dramatic performances were given in honour of the god Dionysus), bringing their tribute money with them. Pericles hoped that they would be enthralled by the plays they watched and awed by the beauty of the buildings they saw rapidly rising on the acropolis, and that they would feel it was an honour rather than a disgrace to be subject to such a city.

The Parthenon was, therefore, just one part of the amazing intellectual and artistic flowering that blossomed in Athens in the fifth century BC.

Most of our information about the reactions of people at the

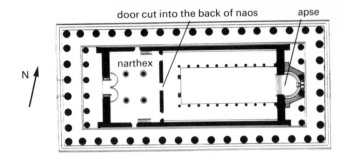

5.1 Plan of the Parthenon after its conversion into a church. The main entrance was now from the west, as was usual for a church. The small western room was turned into the narthex and doors were cut at the back of it leading into the main body of the church. The altar was placed at the eastern end and an apse extended the space behind it. The apse protruded out beyond the original entrance of the Parthenon as far as the columns of the pronaos.

time to Pericles' building projects comes from Plutarch, who lived more than 500 years later. Few books by authors from the time of Pericles have survived and of these, few discuss art. Indirectly, however, the historian Thucydides, who must have been growing up in Athens while the Parthenon was being built, comments with pride on the glory that such works bring a city. He says that if powerful Sparta were deserted and only the temples and foundations of buildings remained, future generations would find it hard to believe that Sparta had been as mighty as she was said to have been; but if the same thing were to happen to Athens, people would think her even greater than she actually was.

And he was right.

The Parthenon under the Romans

For almost a thousand years nothing very important happened in the history of the Parthenon. In the later fourth century BC, Alexander the Great sent some shields that he had captured from the Persians in the battle at the Granicus river to decorate the Parthenon and to recall the Persian invasions of a century and a half before, which he now considered himself to be avenging. The shields were attached to the architrave of the Parthenon (3.26).

By the end of the second century BC Athens had been incorporated, along with the rest of Greece, into the Roman empire. Though technically free, her political importance was lost. However, she still remained a cultural centre and a much respected university town. Intellectual Romans visited Athens, listened to the lectures of the philosophers and gaped at the sights. Only for the Emperor Nero was an inscription in

bronze letters attached to the architrave of the east front of the Parthenon. Otherwise the building was admired and generally left alone.

Occasionally, copies were made of the sculptures of the Parthenon to decorate important public monuments. Souvenir reproductions of the celebrated statue of Athena were manufactured for the Roman tourists to take home with them.

When the Roman empire was threatened by barbarian invasions in the third century AD, Athens too was in peril. In AD 267 the Gothic Herulians overran the lower city. The acropolis was turned into a fortress; this had been its earliest role, long before it had been given over to the worship of the gods, and for nearly another 1600 years it continued as such.

So far the Parthenon had been virtually untouched.

The Parthenon as a church and a mosque

The first major change the Parthenon underwent was its transformation from a pagan temple into a Christian church (5.1), dedicated to the Virgin Mother of Christ. This had probably taken place by the seventh century.

The entrance was changed from the east to the west. The little western back room was turned into the entrance hall (*narthex*) of the church. Doors were cut into the wall that separated the narthex from the naos of the temple, which became the main body of the church. (The colossal statue of Athena had already been removed by the end of the fifth century). An *apse* (a rounded recess) was now built out at the east end of the church. At some point a new high roof was erected over the central part of the main body of the church

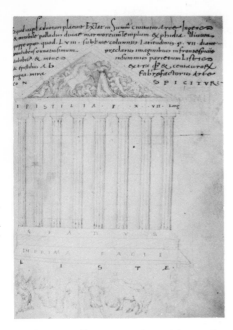

5.2 The west side of the Parthenon copied from a drawing made by the Italian Cyriacus of Ancona on his visit to Greece in the second quarter of the fifteenth century.

5.3 Drawing of the acropolis as it was in 1670. Notice the crenellated tower to the left that was built as part of the 'Frankish' fortifications. The alteration made to the roof of the Parthenon was part of the early Christian remodelling of the temple, when a nave was installed in what had been the naos of the temple. While it was a Christian church, the Parthenon was known as 'Our Lady of Athens'. Could some memory have lingered on of Athena, the original 'Lady' of Athens?

and the walls supporting this roof were pierced with arched windows so that the once dark interior could be flooded with light.

When the Roman empire split into eastern and western parts, Athens naturally belonged to the eastern (Byzantine) empire. After the Fourth Crusade in 1204, she came under the domination of feudal lords from western Europe and the Parthenon was changed from a Greek Orthodox to a Roman Catholic church. It was still dedicated to the Virgin Mary.

The Duchy of Athens, as it came to be in 1260, was governed first by Frankish rulers, then by the adventurous mercenary soldiers of the Catalan Grand Company, and finally by members of a Florentine family called Acciaiuoli. During the rule of the Acciaiuoli, an Italian named Cyriacus of Ancona visited Athens and made some drawings of the Parthenon as it was in the second quarter of the fifteenth century (5.2).

The Renaissance was just beginning in Italy, and Cyriacus knew from ancient literature that he was looking at the temple of Athena. He drew the west end which he, and many after him, mistakenly thought was the front of the temple. After all, it was the entrance to the church.

Cyriacus was obviously impressed by the horses in the ped-

iment, but the drawing is not very accurate (compare it with the seventeenth-century one, 4.18). The proportions too are quite wrong; it is not easy for an untrained person to draw a classical building correctly.

Not long after Cyriacus' visit Athens was conquered by the Turks. Constantinople had fallen to them in 1453 and Athens fell a few years later. The Parthenon was turned into a mosque and the Christian bell tower that had been erected beside it was made into a minaret, but otherwise little was altered.

Few visitors came from the west for the next two centuries, but fortunately some drawings were made in the 1670s (5.3, 4.18 and 4.19).

The explosion of 1687: the Parthenon in ruins

In 1687 the Venetians (following up the defeat of the Turks before Vienna in 1683) besieged the acropolis. The Turks had stored their gunpowder in the Parthenon. Venetian bombardment ignited the powder and there was a tremendous explosion (5.4). The whole centre of the Parthenon was blown

VEDUTA DEL CAST.D ACROPOLIS DALLA PARTE DI TRAMONTANA.

left: *5.4 An engraving showing the explosion when the gunpowder in the Parthenon was detonated in 1687.*

above: *5.5 The Parthenon in 1766 with a small mosque inside it. Notice how many houses had been erected on the acropolis. Marble from the Parthenon (architectural or sculpted) was often built into their walls or sometimes burned for lime which was used as mortar.*

below: *5.6 The condition of the Parthenon in 1804. You can still see the 'Frankish' tower in the distance at the right.*

out, though the ends were relatively undamaged. What had been the best-preserved of all Greek temples now became a ruin.

From time to time people had taken away bits from the Parthenon as souvenirs, but the splendour of the building and its completeness had probably inhibited any extensive plans to despoil it. Such inhibitions were now swept away.

The Venetians had a tradition of carting off works of art from conquered cities to decorate their own. For instance, when they sacked Constantinople in 1204, they took four magnificent bronze horses from the fallen city as an adornment for the church of San Marco. Now they wished to perform a similar feat and carry the great marble horses from the west pediment back in triumph to Venice. While the heavy statues were being lowered, the tackle broke and the sculptures fell and were shattered.

Within a short time the Venetians withdrew from Athens and the Turks reoccupied the city. Nothing much had changed – except the condition of the Parthenon.

After the Venetians left, the Turks built a small mosque within the ruins of the Parthenon. A drawing made in 1766 shows what the acropolis looked like at this time (5.5). Another drawing (5.6), made in 1804, gives a good view of the mosque and shows how devastated the Parthenon was. Smashed bits of sculpture lay about on the ground. Some of them were used as building material, some were burned for lime, and some were carried away by travellers. Much was lost.

The Elgin Marbles

This was the state of affairs when Lord Elgin took up his post as British ambassador to Turkey in 1799.

Lord Elgin assembled a whole company of artists whom he sent to make drawings and casts of the monuments in Athens, particularly the Parthenon. Most of the drawings were lost in a shipwreck, but the casts (an invaluable record) survived.

In the meantime more and more sculpture was being taken from the Parthenon. Before the explosion of 1687 there had been twenty human figures and two horses in the west pediment of the Parthenon (4.18); by 1749 only twelve figures remained and by 1800 only four were left. Lord Elgin was convinced that he should try to rescue the sculptures themselves. If he did not, he feared that they would either be destroyed by time and haphazard vandalism or carried off piecemeal and lost. The French ambassador had also been seeking permission to remove the sculptures from the building. So far it had not been given. Lord Elgin reasoned that if he did not take the sculpture soon, someone else would.

Europe was now in the midst of the Napoleonic wars. The Turks, who had long been friends of the French, were deeply offended when the French army invaded Egypt, then a part of the Turkish empire. When the British drove the French out of Egypt in 1801, Turkish gratitude knew no bounds. Lord Elgin was granted permission to excavate and remove whatever he wished, so long as he did not interfere with any Turkish fortifications.

Lord Elgin's staff seized the opportunity.

A drawing made in 1801 (5.7) shows what the southeast corner of the Parthenon looked like before Lord Elgin's team started the work of removal in earnest. Another picture (5.8) shows what the south side looked like after the metopes on that side had been taken down.

Since the metopes had been slipped into place before the supports for the roof were installed, the reverse process of

above: *5.7 The Parthenon in 1801 seen from the southeast corner. The south side, from which the metopes were removed, runs along towards the left.*

below: *5.8 The south side (towards the east) after the removal of the metopes.*

removing the metopes meant that much of the superstructure had to be taken away before the metopes could be withdrawn. Some of the architecture was thereby destroyed.

Moral judgements are difficult to make in this case. Decay and loss had been severe up to the time of Lord Elgin's arrival and continued afterwards. Comparisons between the casts made by Lord Elgin in the early years of the nineteenth century and photographs of the west frieze (which remained in place on the building) taken less than 100 years later show how much damage continued to occur. Pieces of the frieze, especially heads, kept on disappearing.

Lord Elgin gave his collection of marbles from the Parthenon to the British nation in 1816. He asked only for repayment of his expenses in bringing the sculpture to England. These had been colossal. He received less than half of them and remained deeply in debt for the rest of his life.

At the time when Lord Elgin brought the Parthenon sculptures to England, it was customary to commission a sculptor to complete any fragmentary ancient statues. Heads, arms, and legs were freely added, for neither the public nor even the experts were expected to enjoy the sight of headless women or armless men.

Lord Elgin approached the most celebrated sculptor of his day, the Italian Canova, and asked him to undertake the restorations. Canova declined, and he is reported to have said that however greatly it was to be lamented that these statues should have suffered so much from time and barbarism yet it was undeniable that they had never been retouched, that they were the work of the ablest artists the world had ever seen ... 'it would be sacrilege' in him or any other man to presume to touch them with a chisel.

The reaction of other artists to the sculptures of the Parthenon was, like Canova's, immediate and overwhelmingly enthusiastic. Many of the experts and connoisseurs of ancient art agreed with the artists, but others were slower to respond.

They had been accustomed to the smooth, sleek forms popular in Greece in the fourth century BC and later, and the power of the Parthenon sculptures took them by surprise.

Lord Elgin had hoped that the presence of the marbles would lead to a great blossoming of art in England. His hopes do not seem to have been realized. The artists who took inspiration from the Parthenon sculptures were not great ones and the ways in which the marbles were adapted and used seem rather trivial, as for instance in the frieze of the Athenaeum Club in London.

The present: the Parthenon in danger again

Within five years of the installation of the sculptures from the Parthenon in the British Museum, the Greeks rebelled against the Turks in a war of national liberation.

In 1833 the Turks withdrew from Athens. The acropolis, which they had used as a stronghold, was surrendered. The Greeks decided that it should never again be a fortress – or even a residence. (Some people thought the royal palace should be built there, but the new king of Greece modestly declined the suggestion.)

The acropolis was given over to history – ancient history. The Greeks, now at last free from foreign domination, insisted on destroying all post-classical buildings. There had been 300 houses on the acropolis and numerous Byzantine, Frankish, and Turkish additions and modifications. All were doomed. The Greek Archaeological Service took over the acropolis and proceeded with excavations and reconstructions.

Excavations (particularly after 1885) were carried all the way down to bedrock, beneath even the classical surface of the acropolis (though the major classical buildings were left undisturbed). Ruins and statues that had been buried before the time of Pericles emerged. Pieces of sculpture that had fallen from the Parthenon centuries before were recovered. A law was passed forbidding anyone to take antiquities out of the country. Fragments of ancient sculpture found in the area are now kept in the Acropolis Museum.

The work of re-erecting the walls and columns of the Parthenon was begun in 1842, but only really got under way in the twentieth century. It was completed in 1933.

Although the engineer in charge from 1895 knew that the ancient Greeks had always encased their iron clamps in lead (3.16) in order to seal them off from air and moisture, he did not do this himself with sufficient care; he also placed too much faith in the steel bars that he used for reinforcement. The results were disastrous.

By the 1970s the new metal clamps had begun to rust and swell and thereby threaten to split the marble in which they were embedded. Those that could be found and removed have been replaced with clamps made of bronze or stainless steel. Others had to be sought by means of gamma-rays emitted from a cobalt source, which also located cracks which could then be treated. The procedure is rather like taking X-ray photographs of the temple.

Now, too, another problem emerged: air pollution. Buildings which had withstood two and a half thousand years of rain, hail and sleet began to crumble under the action of sulphur dioxide carried in industrial fumes and the smoke from central heating systems. New laws were passed to control air pollution around the acropolis, but much damage had already been done.

In order to save what was left, the last three statues in the west pediment of the Parthenon were removed (5.9) to the Acropolis Museum in 1976. Thus the Greek Archaeological Service took the final step in the process of denuding the pediment, a process that had begun after the Venetian explosion almost 300 years before.

In 1977 UNESCO (the United Nations Educational, Scientific, and Cultural Organization) launched an international campaign to rescue the historic monuments on the acropolis, threatened as they are by the steady march of tourists' feet, by the destructive expansion of the clamps used to hold them together, and even by the very air around them.

When the Parthenon stood fresh and new in all its splendour and glory, Pericles proudly boasted to the Athenians: 'Mighty indeed are the marks and monuments of our empire. Future ages will wonder at us, as the present age wonders at us now.'

Bold, prophetic words they proved to be.

5.9 Lord Elgin removed one of the statues from the west pediment; the rest were taken down by the Greek Archaeological Service. The photograph shows two of them packed up so that they can be lowered from the pediment. Plastic copies, made with the help of the British Museum, have been put in their place.

Glossary

acroteria (singular: acroterion) decorative ornaments placed above the three angles of the pediment (3.26)

anathyrosis the strip of smooth finish given to the sides and top of the vertical joining surfaces of wall blocks (3.16). The same term can be used of the horizontal joining surfaces of column drums (3.10)

antefix (plural: antefixes) vertical decoration attached to the ends of the cover-tiles on the long sides of the roof (3.24–3.26)

apse a rounded recess, usually behind the altar in a church (5.1)

architrave a lintel or beam carried from the top of one column to another (2.14, 2.15)

capital top part of a column, crowning the shaft and supporting the architrave (2.14, 2.15)

chryselephantine technique of covering a wooden statue with plates of gold and strips of ivory

column vertical support, circular in section, consisting of shaft and capital (and, in the Ionic order, also a base) (2.14, 2.15)

column drums stone cylinders of which the shaft of a column is composed (3.7, 3.10)

dentils small tooth-like features used as an alternative to a continuous frieze in the Ionic order (2.13)

dipteral having a double peristyle (2.12, 2.13)

Doric order an architectural system controlling the design of column and entablature (pages 14–15 and 2.14)

entablature the superstructure carried by the columns. It consisted of architrave (resting directly on the columns), frieze (in the middle) and projecting cornice, including gutter (at the top) (2.14, 2.15)

entasis the slight convex curve given to the tapering of columns in order to avoid the severe impression (or even concave appearance) that would come of using absolutely straight lines (page 26)

epistatai members of a committee of five overseers who supervised how funds voted for public building projects in Athens were spent (page 8)

flutes vertical channels carved in the shafts of columns (page 15)

free-standing statues those carved fully in the round, entirely detached from any background

frieze the horizontal bands of stone resting on top of the architrave, the Doric frieze being divided into triglyphs and metopes, the Ionic frieze being continuous (2.14, 2.15)

interaxial distance from the centre of one column to the centre of the next

Ionians a branch of the Greek people speaking an Ionian dialect of Greek (as opposed to Dorian or Aeolian) and living mostly on the west coast of Asia Minor, the islands of the Aegean, and Athens

Ionic order an architectural system controlling the design of column and entablature (page 15 and 2.15)

metope stone panel inserted between pairs of triglyphs in the Doric frieze (2.14, 4.3–4.6)

naos the central, inner part of a Greek temple, where the statue of the god was kept (Latin equivalent, *cella*)

narthex enclosed passage between the main entrance and the nave of a church (5.1)

palmette stylized floral decoration consisting of an odd number of petal-shaped forms of which the central one is the tallest

Panathenaia annual Athenian festival in honour of the goddess Athena, celebrated with special pomp and elaboration every four years

pediment triangular end of a gabled roof which could be filled with sculpture (4.1, 4.18–4.21)

peplos Greek woman's dress made from a rectangular piece of cloth pinned at the shoulders

peripteral having a peristyle (2.10, 2.11)

peristyle colonnade that surrounds all four sides of a Greek temple

Persepolis site of a grand palace and administrative centre of the Persian kings

post and lintel structural system by which vertical posts (columns or walls) support horizontal lintels (architraves or ceilings) (2.16)

pronaos porch in front of the naos of a temple

relief sculpture which is attached to a background, either very deeply carved (high relief) as on the metopes of the Parthenon, or shallowly carved (low relief) as on the frieze of the Parthenon

stylobate top step of a temple, the platform on which the columns rest

triglyphs vertically grooved parts of the Doric frieze (2.14)

volutes spiral scrolls decorating the front and back of Ionic capitals (2.15)

Index

Acknowledgments

The author and publisher would like to thank the following for permission to reproduce illustrations:
front cover Peter Baker Photography; title page R. Schoder, SJ; 1.2, 2.9, 2.11, 3.13, 4.8, 4.14 Hirmer Fotoarchiv München; 1.3, 3.7, 3.11, 3.21, 3.28, 4.7, 4.10, 4.15, 4.17, back cover Susan Woodford; 1.4, 2.1, 2.2, 2.3, 2.5, 4.1, 4.3, 4.4, 4.11, 4.12, 4.18, 4.19, 4.20, 4.21, 5.4, 5.5, 5.7, 5.8 reproduced by Courtesy of the Trustees of the British Museum; 2.4 Kunsthistorisches Museum, Vienna; 2.6, 2.8, 2.12, 2.15, 2.16, 3.10, 3.24 drawn by Susan Bird, courtesy of the Trustees of the British Museum; 2.7 Radio Times Hulton Picture Library; 3.19 George Braziller Inc (from R. Scranton, *Greek Architecture*, 1965); 2.13 Royal Institute of British Architects; 2.14 Batsford (from A. Stratton, *The Orders of Architecture*, 1931); 2.17, 3.1, 3.2, 3.20, 3.22, 3.23, 3.29 Granada (from J. J. Coulton, *Greek Architects at Work*, Elek, 1977); 2.18, 3.8, 3.9, 3.15, 3.16, 3.17, 3.18, 4.22 from R. Martin, *Manuel d'Architecture Greque I Materiaux et Techniques*, Picard et Cie, 1965; 3.3 Paul White; 3.4, 4.6 Deutsches Archaeologisches Institut, Athens; 3.6, 3.14 Alison Frantz; 3.12 Oxford University Press (from A. Burford, 'Builders of the Parthenon', *Greece and Rome* supp. to vol X, 1963); 3.25, 3.26, 4.13 American School of Classical Studies at Athens; 3.27 reproduced from the *Architecture of Ancient Greece* by William Dinsmoor, by permission of W. W. Norton and Company, Inc. © 1975 by W. W. Norton and Company Inc.; 4.2 from *Rivista dell'Istituto Nazionale d'Archaeologia e Storia dell'Arte* NS IV (1955) figs 24 and 25; 4.5 Eva-Maria Stresow-Czakó; 4.16 Sylvia A. Matheson Schofield; 5.1 from J. Travlos, *Pictorial Dictionary of Ancient Athens*, Thames & Hudson, 1971; 5.2 Deutsche Staatsbibliothek Berlin, DDR; 5.3 Akademisches Kuntsmuseum der Universität, Bonn; 5.6 Österreichische Nationalbibliothek; 5.9 Ministry of Culture and Science, Athens; 3.5 Archaeological Institute of America.

Map by Reg Piggott

front cover: *The Parthenon and the acropolis from the southwest.*

back cover: *The Parthenon from the northwest.*

title page: *The acropolis of Athens seen from the air. The large ruined building in the centre of the photograph is the Parthenon. The other buildings on the acropolis were created later, as was also the present form of the theatre of Dionysus, visible in the lower right corner.*

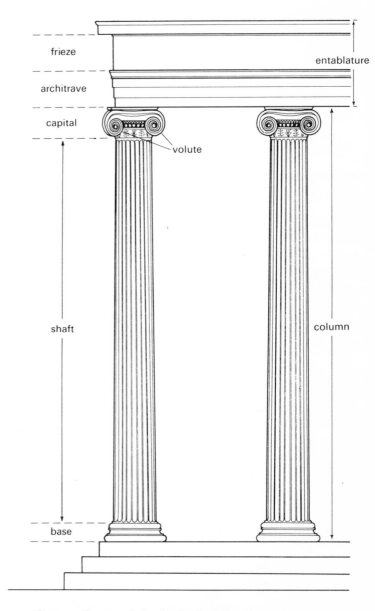

Corner of a temple in the Ionic order.

The Cambridge History Library

The Cambridge Introduction to History
Written by Trevor Cairns

PEOPLE BECOME CIVILIZED   EUROPE AND THE WORLD

THE ROMANS AND THEIR EMPIRE   THE BIRTH OF MODERN EUROPE

BARBARIANS, CHRISTIANS, AND MUSLIMS   THE OLD REGIME AND THE REVOLUTION

THE MIDDLE AGES   POWER FOR THE PEOPLE

EUROPE AROUND THE WORLD

The Cambridge Topic Books
General Editor Trevor Cairns

THE AMERICAN WAR OF INDEPENDENCE   LIFE IN A MEDIEVAL VILLAGE

BENIN: AN AFRICAN KINGDOM AND CULTURE   LIFE IN THE IRON AGE

THE BUDDHA   LIFE IN THE OLD STONE AGE

BUILDING THE MEDIEVAL CATHEDRALS   THE MAORIS

CHINA AND MAO ZEDONG   MARTIN LUTHER

CHRISTOPHER WREN
AND ST. PAUL'S CATHEDRAL   MEIJI JAPAN

THE MURDER OF ARCHBISHOP THOMAS

THE EARLIEST FARMERS AND THE FIRST CITIES   MUSLIM SPAIN

EARLY CHINA AND THE WALL   THE NAVY THAT BEAT NAPOLEON

THE FIRST SHIPS AROUND THE WORLD   THE PARTHENON

GANDHI AND THE STRUGGLE
FOR INDIA'S INDEPENDENCE   POMPEII

THE PYRAMIDS

HERNAN CORTES: CONQUISTADOR IN MEXICO   THE ROMAN ARMY

HITLER AND THE GERMANS   THE ROMAN ENGINEERS

THE INDUSTRIAL REVOLUTION BEGINS   ST. PATRICK AND IRISH CHRISTIANITY

LIFE IN A FIFTEENTH-CENTURY MONASTERY   THE VIKING SHIPS

The Cambridge History Library will be expanded in the future to include additional volumes. Lerner Publications Company is pleased to participate in making this excellent series of books available to a wide audience of readers.

Lerner Publications Company
241 First Avenue North, Minneapolis, Minnesota 55401